# STEVEN UNIVERSE

## GUIDE TO THE CRYSTAL GEMS

by Rebecca Sugar

CARTOON NETWORK BOOKS

An Imprint of Penguin Random House

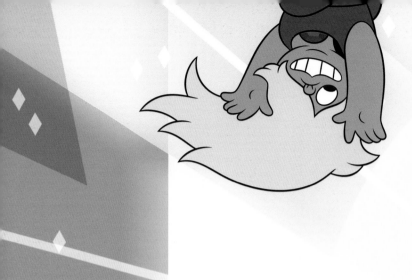

CARTOON NETWORK BOOKS
Penguin Young Readers Group
An Imprint of Penguin Random House LLC

ISBN 978-0-8431-8316-0

10 9 8 7 6 5 4 3 2 1

There are a lot of people in this world who don't fit in, and might act strange, and tend to keep to themselves. That's definitely true of the Crystal Gems, who aren't even people at all! They're aliens who have chosen to live on Earth, and they're devoted to protecting the human race!

But as much as they love humans, they don't really know how to act around them. Steven Quartz Universe, the youngest Crystal Gem, is the only half human on the team, so he's easily the best at interacting with humans! He also knows the Gems really well and why they are the way they are.

He wrote this guide, so that if you ever come across Garnet, Amethyst, Pearl, or any of their Fusions, or even Gems from Homeworld, you'll know how to talk to them.

All right, Steven Universe, take it from here!

—REBECCA SUGAR
Creator of Steven Universe

# TABLE OF CONTENTS

Hello, human beings!
I'm Steven Quartz Universe! I look pretty human, but I'm actually half Gem, on my mom's side. Aside from my dad, most humans don't know much about Gems, which is a real shame, because there are a lot of interesting things I think everybody ought to know about Gems, especially the Crystal Gems. We're right here on Earth, and we love you, and we want to keep you safe!

Gems are a species, but the Crystal Gems are a movement! Five thousand five hundred years ago, we fought for this planet's independence! Thanks to the tireless efforts of the fearless, brilliant, incomparable Rose Quartz, this is NOT a Gem-controlled planet!

Mom and the Crystal Gems already saved the world!

Yes! There was just so much on Earth that was worth protecting!

4

5

Amethyst actually joined the team after the fight for Earth. Mom found her in a big, rocky place called the Kindergarten. That's the place where Amethyst was made! There are lots of holes that other Gems came out of, too. Amethyst's hole is still there!

The Kindergarten is kind of scary, but Amethyst isn't—she's really fun. I think it's cool that she's a Gem but she's an earthling, too! Maybe that's why she likes eating and sleeping and doing lots of human stuff, even though Gems don't need to do anything like that. I think even if I was full Gem, I'd still wanna do all that stuff, too!

Amethyst is really strong, and she has a whip, and she likes to shape-shift a lot—she's really good at that—and she has a huge junk collection! Anyway, Amethyst is really, really cool . . .

Garnet is our leader! She's the strongest fighter, and she can see visions of the future, which help the team figure out what to do! She's really tough and really nice, and she's a FUSION! Gems can do a thing where they dance and glow, and then their bodies kind of phase into each other, and they turn into a totally new Gem with a whole new personality and everything!

For a lot of Gems, that's really hard to do, but it's not for Garnet, because Garnet wants to stay together. She's made of Ruby and Sapphire, two Gems who love each other and can't stand to be apart! That's why Garnet is so strong—she's made of love, and it's really, really strong! Maybe that's why she's so great at being a leader, because she doesn't think just one person knows better—she really believes in teamwork, and she listens to all of us. That's probably also why she's so quiet. Maybe she's just talking things over and listening inside herself all the time! Or maybe she's looking into the future. Anyway, I love Garnet.

9

Pearl is amazing! Pearl is really strong and really smart and a really good fighter! She was with Mom for a long time, and they fought for Earth together. She knows all about Gem history, and I think she really misses space, but she chose Earth, and she's still here protecting it— and protecting me, too!

Pearl worries about everything and everybody, but it's all okay. I know it's because she wants everything to be perfect. That's why she tries so hard to be the best at everything she does.

She makes me want to try hard, too, and be better than I am now, and make her proud! I think she feels a little bad when things don't go exactly like she wants them to, but I don't care about that. I just care about Pearl!

Fight for life on the planet Earth,

Defend all human beings, even the ones that you don't understand,

Believe in love that is out of anyone's control,

And then risk everything for it!

Even though we've already won the fight for Earth, we're still trying to keep it safe! There are battle-damaged Gems that are still around, and they're not like us. Something's really wrong with them. They're like horrible monsters. We have to poof their bodies away, and then we keep their Gems inside of bubbles, so they can't form again and hurt anybody. Maybe someday I'll be able to heal what's wrong with them, but I'm not sure how. Mom couldn't fix them, either. For now we're keeping them safe inside the Temple.

There are new Gems, too, coming back here from the Gem Homeworld . . . They don't really care about the Earth or humans, and they don't seem to like us Crystal Gems much at all. But don't worry, whatever they want to do to the Earth, we'll stop them!

We're doing our best!

Please don't be afraid.

We've got this!

# Steven Quartz Universe

**Species:** Human-Gem hybrid
**Gem Type:** Quartz
**Alignment:** Crystal Gems
**Hair Color:** Curly black
**Clothing:** Pink T-shirt with a gold star, blue jeans, and pink flip-flops
**Gem:** Rose quartz (inherited from his mother)
**Gem Location:** Belly
**Weapon:** Shield
**Fun Fact:** Steven wasn't made like other Gems—he's the first and only Gem to ever be born!
**Favorite Quote:** "BOOOOKS!"

I'm pretty cool, I guess! I really like being a human and a Gem at the same time. I have powers, and I get to live with Garnet and Amethyst and Pearl, but I still get to see Dad all the time, and I get to know a lot of humans . . .

I really want to understand everybody, and I think I can, because even if I'm not like anybody, I also *am* like *everybody*! Oh, and I'm really good at music, because Dad taught me how to play a bunch of instruments. I really like to draw, too, and I'm getting better at it every day.

And even though I've figured out how to do lots of Gem stuff, I still have a lot to learn. All the other Crystal Gems have been doing Gem stuff for thousands of years longer than me, so I'm not that worried. I'm just getting started, and I know I'll get the hang of everything.

# How Is It Possible?!

Rose Quartz was determined to bridge the gap between Gems and humanity. We are not humans, but we *can* create an amazingly accurate simulation of a human body via shape-shifting. This can allow us to experiment with human experience; we can make lungs and experience breathing, or a stomach and experience eating. Rose Quartz wanted to experience birth.

Usually Gems are made, not born! Colorful goo stuff is put super deep in the ground, and after lotsa time and pressure, a Gem gets formed. When we're ready, we glow and make a body for the first time, and pop out of the ground! We come out just like we are, and then pretty much stay that way forever. We don't have to bother growing up like humans do!

But Rose Quartz wanted to create a *human* child. One who could learn and grow, with the capacity for love that comes so naturally to human beings.

A Gem *is* their Gem. Our physical forms generate from our Gems. All the information that makes us who we are is sourced in the Gem itself. To give that information to a human child, Rose Quartz was able to integrate her information with the DNA of Greg Universe by dissipating her physical form to allow all of her Gem's information to become half of Steven's self.

Not unlike a Fusion, Rose disappeared to create an entirely new being, with all of her self integrated into half of his self. Steven is, in essence, a Fusion of love, like me!

And an earthling, like me!

And one of a kind, like Rose Quartz!

Human stuff comes easy to me! Sleeping and eating and breathing and stuff! The Gems don't really get it, but they totally try to. They always cut me slack when I can't do things they can do, and they'll watch TV, and play video games with me, and sing and play music, too.

# Gem Powers

I can make a Rose Quartz shield! Dad told me that Mom used this shield to protect everybody back in the day.

I can also make a Rose Quartz bubble! I can bubble myself and my friends, to keep them safe. I'm really good at this one! I can also make small bubbles around Gems to contain them.

I've got healing spit! But it doesn't always work. I healed Lapis Lazuli's Gem, and I fixed Dad's leg, but some things I just can't fix. I think I get psyched out . . . Maybe it only works on living beings? I'm not sure!

I can fuse! I haven't fused with any of the Gems yet, but I've fused with Connie! A Gem has never been able to fuse with a human before, but the Gems think I can because I'm half human! Being a Fusion is amazing— you kind of disappear, but somehow you're still there, and when you both know what to do, and what you want, and support each other, you get so much stronger than just one person on their own!

# Garnet

**Species:** Gem
**Gem Type:** Fusion
**Alignment:** Crystal Gem
**Hair Color:** Black
**Clothing:** Black, red, and purple bodysuit. Cool purple shades to shield her third eye. Large shoulder pads, and a pink star on her chest.
**Gem Location:** Palms
**Weapon:** Gauntlets that she conjures from the gems on her hands
**Fun Fact:** When Ruby and Sapphire first formed Garnet, it was very unusual for two different types of Gems to form a Fusion.
**Favorite Quote:** "I am made of love, and it's stronger than you!"

24

# Always Together

Garnet is super cool all the time! She's got all the answers! Sometimes she's pretty quiet, but it's probably because she's always thinking about the future, since she can see a bunch of it! That's the Sapphire part of Garnet . . . but Garnet is also really fierce and tough, and can fight and beat anything! She likes to solve problems by punching them. She's so hard-core . . . that's the Ruby part of Garnet! But she's also honest, super strong, and so sure about everything . . . that's the love part of Garnet!

Ruby seems really tough. She's got a hot temper and gets really frustrated when she's separated from Sapphire. She might rush into things without thinking, but she can't help it—she needs to take action! She cares about Sapphire more than anything.

Sapphire seems really calm. Even when she was in trouble, she sensed that Ruby would come for her! She's really deep and thoughtful—maybe a little quiet and a little distant—but when it comes to Ruby, Sapphire acts really fast, because she knows exactly what she wants: for them to always be together!

# Fearless Leader

We always look to Garnet when we need to know what to do next!

Good one.

Yes, Garnet has a real hands-on approach!

I get it! Hands . . . hands-on approach! 'Cause her Gems are on her hands!

Why yes, thank you. I was working on that all morning.

Garnet can be a little . . . blunt! Maybe a little forward sometimes, and maybe a little reserved other times, by human standards.

If you talk to her, just try to remember she probably has a lot going on inside of herself. She definitely doesn't mean to be rude or confusing! She doesn't really do chitchat, so cut straight to real talk if you're talking to Garnet. She'll probably have some really great relationship advice, if you need it!

# Fearsome Foes

Garnet has fought and bubbled lots of corrupted Gems!

Garnet kept up with Lapis Lazuli's water clone!

Jasper couldn't keep Garnet apart!

# ★ Memorable Moments ★

Garnet's logic helps keep me calm when
I start to freak out!

Garnet liked the special outfit I picked for the Gems' birthday party. I think it suits her!

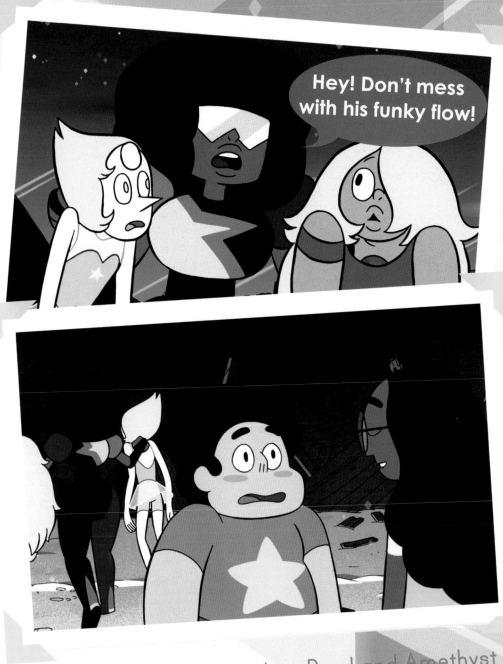

Garnet helps out when Pearl and Amethyst try to embarrass me!

Even though Garnet may not get *my* jokes, sometimes she's really funny, too!

Oops! Sometimes Garnet takes things kind of literally.

People can get really confused by things Garnet says!

Connie's mom wouldn't let her come over for a while after this . . .

# Amethyst

**Species:** Gem
**Gem Type:** Quartz
**Alignment:** Crystal Gem
**Hair Color:** Pale lavender
**Clothing:** Leggings with stars on the knees and an oversize tank top
**Gem Location:** Chest
**Weapon:** Whip
**Fun Fact:** Amethyst has experimented with male forms, including wrestling alter ego the Purple Puma
**Favorite Quote:** "Who needs to go see movies when you've got MAGIC?"

Amethyst is the youngest Gem, aside from me! Sure, she's thousands of years old, but she didn't come out of the ground until after Garnet and Pearl and Mom were already done fighting the Earth war. Maybe it's good that she missed it—I'm glad she was safe in the ground while it was all going on. Amethyst's like me: She's never been to the Gem Homeworld or space or anything, but that's just fine, because Earth is totally the best!

Amethyst is a crazy good fighter—she can turn into a big wrestler and roll super fast into things like a big tire, and she can grab things and throw things and even cut things with her whip!

# She's Probably Just Kidding!

Amethyst can pull pranks sometimes, and she might even seem a little mean if you don't know her that well, but she's probably just kidding! If you can handle her making fun of you a little, you'll see. She's hilarious, her room is full of more cool stuff than you can even imagine, and she can eat just about anything and turn into anything, too. Nobody is more fun to hang out with than Amethyst!

# Fearsome Foes

Amethyst can almost hold her own against Garnet!

That is no small thing.

She lost against Lapis Lazuli's water clone . . .

But she totally beat Peridot on the Hand Ship!

# ★ Memorable Moments ★

Greg is . . . nice, Steven, but I doubt Rose would entrust him with a powerful weapon like the Light Cannon.

Your dad's kind of a mess, Steven.

Amethyst's not afraid of tellin' it like it is! (But my dad's actually pretty cool.)

Amethyst has a lot of old junk! This is probably why
Pearl doesn't like to go into Amethyst's room.

This is the time that I saved us from a bunch of crystal shrimp by feeding them bagel sandwiches! Amethyst made fun of me a little, but I'm pretty sure she was impressed.

Amethyst tried to teach me to shape-shift into a cat, like her, but instead I just got cat fingers. Oh well!

Amethyst doesn't lose her cool, even when she probably should!

Sometimes it's hard to tell when Amethyst is messing with me. I'm pretty sure she was messing with me . . .

Amethyst and Pearl disagree sometimes, but I know they care about each other!

# Pearl

**Species:** Gem
**Gem Type:** Pearl
**Alignment:** Crystal Gem
**Hair Color:** Pink
**Clothing:** Blue leotard with a tiny gold star on the front, and a ribbon around her waist. Pink socks and pale blue flats.
**Gem Location:** Forehead
**Weapon:** Spear
**Fun Fact:** Pearl is able to project holographic images from her Gem.
**Favorite Quote:** "Humans find such fascinating ways to waste their time."

# In the Name of Rose Quartz

Pearl has been fighting for Earth for a really, really long time! She and Mom were the original Crystal Gems. When Mom first decided to stay on Earth to try to save it, Pearl stayed, too, because she didn't want to leave Mom. Now Pearl's got a ton of amazing stories from the war, and a huge collection of swords, and she's still fighting to protect Earth, even after all these years. Pearl and Mom were really close. She always tells me about how amazing Mom was. She probably knows more about Mom than anybody, maybe even Dad.

# Hard Work and Dedication . . .

Pearl works really hard to be a great fighter!
She can shoot laser blasts out of her spear, and she
knows all sorts of super-difficult sword fighting moves!

I may not have been
made for fighting . . .
but that's what
technique is for!

You always were
a force on the
battlefield.

Oh, yes, well, one
does try one's best!

# She Really Does Care About You!

Pearl has a hard time understanding humans and human stuff, but I know she really tries to be open to it! If she has a hard time talking to you, it's not because she doesn't like you—she just isn't quite sure how to act around people sometimes. I think she's just spent a lot more time around Gems and Gem culture than she's spent around human beings. You should show Pearl all the stuff you like and tell her all about yourself! Even if she seems confused, she's definitely really interested. After all, she's dedicated to protecting humans and the Earth!

Pearl did her best against a giant bird!

She took down Sugilite when Garnet and Amethyst got carried away!

She took on Lapis's water clones with two spears!

Pearl makes sure the rest of us follow the rules!

I just want everyone to know, my plan would have also worked.

Pearl really likes to be right, which is okay, because she usually is! Except when I'm right. Or Garnet. Or Amethyst.

Pearl wanted to teach me proper manners, but I just
wanted to stop sneezing!

61

I think Pearl had a really good time at Funland!

Pearl did her best to explain Gem Fusion to me, but it didn't make sense until I saw it in person!

It was a joke, Pearl! I promise!

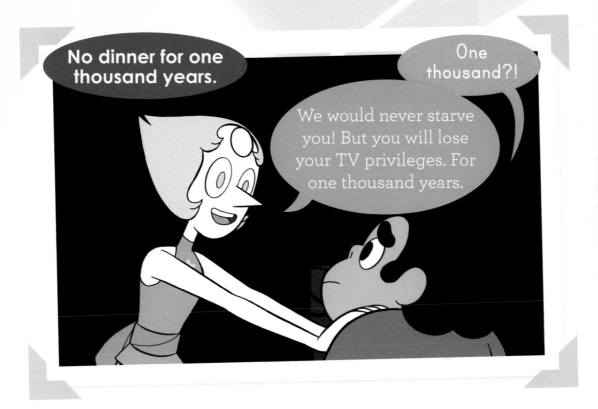

I can't decide if Pearl's punishment is actually any better than Garnet's! No TV?!

# Rose Quartz

**Species:** Gem
**Gem Type:** Quartz
**Alignment:** Crystal Gem, of course!
**Hair Color:** Long pink ringlets
**Clothing:** White dress with a star-shaped cutout on the front to reveal her Gem
**Gem Location:** Belly
**Weapon:** Shield
**Fun Fact:** Rose had a beautiful laugh.
**Favorite Quote:** "I need you to know that every moment you love being yourself, that's me, loving you and loving being you, because you're going to be something extraordinary ... You're going to be a human being."

# The Beauty in Everything

Mom saw the beauty in everything! She really loved humans and all human stuff, and also plants and animals and everything on Earth, I think. And she really loved music, and she really loved Dad. Dad gave her a Mr. Universe shirt after she came to one of his concerts, and she kept it! I saw it hanging up inside Lion's mane. The Gems say I'm a lot like Mom, so I'll take their word for it. I do like Earth . . . and music . . . and shirts, too!

# Half of Me

I have Mom's Gem, and Gems need their Gem to exist, so we can't both exist at the same time. Now all of Mom is half of me. I think you're kind of like that, too: You're half your mom and half your dad, in a DNA kinda way, but since you're both at once, and 'cause you have your own life, you're somebody else who's totally new! I think that's what's going on with me . . . half of me really *is* Mom—she's not gone—but half of me really is Dad, because I'm a human, too, and that's how human kids are. So I'm Mom, and I'm Dad, but mostly I'm me . . . I don't know, writing it out, it seems kind of like a given . . . Well . . . it's something that I think about a lot.

Even though I'll never get to meet my mom in person, I've found some things that help me get to know what she was like! One time, I went into her old room, and it was all pink and fluffy and full of clouds, and I made a cute tiny pink whale appear. The whale talked to me, and the room gave me whatever I asked for! But I think I need some practice to figure out how to make her room work right.

There's a big fountain that looks like Mom in her old
healing spring. She looks like she was a really nice
person, like she cares about everybody so much. For a
while, her fountain was broken and covered with lots of
thorny vines, but then Garnet and Pearl blasted them
all away so that my mom's fountain could work again! I
even thought for a second that her statue moved, but it
must've been my imagination.

I also have a friend, Lion. He's a lion! He definitely used to belong to Mom. And I can phase through his mane! Inside of him is a field with a hill and a tree—that's where I found a bunch of my mom's old stuff. I even found a video that my mom made for me before I was born! I think my mom used Lion to carry her things around, like a living bag. But, of course, Lion's a lot cooler than a bag. He's a mystery—even to Pearl and Amethyst and Garnet!

# Leader of the Crystal Gems

Pearl and Garnet told me about how Mom was the leader of the Crystal Gems back in the day, and how she rebelled against the Gem Homeworld to keep Earth from becoming a Gem-controlled planet. Earth is an independent planet because of Mom. I know everybody used to listen to Mom and look up to her! I hope I can be a great leader like Mom someday.

# No Such Thing as a Good War

Dad said that during the war for Earth, Mom had to turn on her own kind. She had to because Gems were making Kindergartens that were damaging the ground, and if they'd kept making them, it would have wiped out all life on Earth. Mom must have fought really hard. I can tell from her stuff. There are tons of weapons in her armory, extra cannons and axes and armor, and she has a really big sword that I found inside of Lion. I'm glad the Crystal Gems won, but I wish Gems wouldn't fight each other.

# HOMEWORLD GEMS

# Lapis Lazuli

**Species:** Gem
**Gem Type:** Lapis lazuli
**Alignment:** Homeworld Gem
**Hair Color:** Dark blue
**Clothing:** A long skirt and a halter top tied with a ribbon. She is barefoot.
**Gem Location:** Back
**Weapon:** Water
**Fun Fact:** Lapis Lazuli can manifest wings made of water and use them to fly.
**Favorite Quote:** "I just want to go home."

# Peridot

**Species:** Gem
**Gem Type:** Peridot
**Alignment:** Homeworld Gem
**Hair Color:** Pale yellow green
**Clothing:** Green uniform with yellow diamond insignia, and metallic arm and leg enhancements
**Gem Location:** Forehead
**Weapon:** Modern Gem technology
**Fun Fact:** Her fingers can separate from her hand and form a screen that displays her data.
**Favorite Quote:** "You clods!"

# Jasper

**Species:** Gem
**Gem Type:** Quartz
**Alignment:** Homeworld Gem
**Hair Color:** Beige
**Clothing:** Red uniform with yellow diamond insignia, heavy boots, and cape
**Gem Location:** Nose
**Weapon:** Helmet, and Gem destabilizer
**Fun Fact:** Jasper fought against the Crystal Gems 5,500 years ago in the war for Earth.
**Favorite Quote:** "Don't think you've won!"

Hey, Garnet! You should field the Fusion section, don't you think?!

# FUSIONS

Fusion occurs when two or more Gems merge their physical forms into a single new being bearing the multiple Gems of the fusers. Unless the fusers are identical, this new being, their Fusion, will be someone entirely new, with their own color, personality, and powers. A Fusion is more than just a mash-up of the fusers; a Fusion is also a manifestation of the fusers' influence on each other. For example: Ruby is hot. Sapphire is cool. I am electric.

# Living Relationships

A Fusion is a relationship. Some relationships are healthy and stable, like me. Some relationships are unsustainable, even if they seem promising at first. Some are furiously short, some are dangerously long. Some are toxic mistakes that are best avoided. Some are wonderful surprises that open you up to new ways of thinking and being.

Two Gems are always stronger than one if they're willing to work together. But a truly great Fusion is like a truly great relationship: Its power is amplified by trust, respect, absolute honesty, and constant communication.

# Opal

**Species:** Gem
**Gem Type:** Fusion
**Hair Color:** Long white hair in a ponytail, and two small pigtails in the front
**Clothing:** Light green top with a drape in the front and the back, pink leggings, and yellow boots
**Gem Location:** Forehead and chest
**Weapon:** Bow and arrow
**Fun Fact:** Opal is very forgetful.
**Favorite Quote:** "All you wanna do is see me turn into a giant woman."

Amethyst and Pearl are extremely powerful when they're willing to work together in the form of Opal. Amethyst's ability to live in the moment plus Pearl's obsessive single-mindedness result in a Fusion that is very balanced. Opal achieves a peace in that balance that Amethyst and Pearl rarely experience on their own. Such peace, in fact, that Opal can sometimes completely forget what she's supposed to be doing.

Perfect balance is very difficult to hold. It doesn't take much to make Opal fall back into Amethyst and Pearl.

# Sugilite

**Species:** Gem
**Gem Type:** Fusion
**Hair Color:** Dark purple black
**Clothing:** Dark purple, burgundy, and black bodysuit with tears in it, and a visor to cover four of her five eyes
**Gem Location:** Chest and palms
**Weapon:** Flail
**Fun Fact:** Sugilite is a bit of a show-off.
**Favorite Quote:** "Hey, Steven, wanna see something cool?"

# Garnet & Amethyst

Amethyst can be a bit reckless, and I can be a bit brash. At times, we can both get carried away, especially if we're egging each other on. Together we become Sugilite, an uninhibited powerhouse with nothing to prove and everything to show off. Amethyst's lack of inhibition and my raw power make Sugilite so fun to be that it's hard to want to separate once we form her.

In Amethyst's defense, it is very difficult to form a balanced Fusion with yours truly. I'm already two Gems. Three becomes a bit of a party.

# Alexandrite

**Species:** Gem
**Gem Type:** Fusion
**Hair Color:** Aqua blue
**Clothing:** A teal bodysuit with a dark pink belt, and large shoulder plates that are dark purple. Teal, light purple, and dark pink long gloves cover her six arms. There is a dark pink star on each knee of her bodysuit.
**Gem Location:** Forehead, chest, and palms
**Weapon:** All of them
**Fun Fact:** Alexandrite has two functioning mouths.
**Favorite Quote:** "You two, come out of that bus this instant!"

# Garnet, Amethyst & Pearl

Alexandrite is an incredible force on the battlefield. When Pearl, Amethyst, and I fuse together with a singular goal, we are unstoppable. But when the singular goal is a dinner party with a human family, we are very confused, and we are very confusing, and we are very sorry.

# Malachite

**Species:** Gem
**Gem Type:** Fusion
**Hair Color:** Pale green
**Clothing:** Stretched halter top and uniform with yellow diamond insignia
**Gem Location:** Nose
**Weapon:** Water
**Fun Fact:** Malachite is so unstable that she does not have a single voice.
**Favorite Quote:** "Let's stay on this miserable planet together!"

# Lapis & Jasper

These two are really bad for each other. Malachite was formed through extortion and deception, and held together out of revenge. Malachite is the worst relationship imaginable.

# Stevonnie

**Species:** Three-quarters human, one-quarter Gem
**Gem Type:** Hybrid Fusion
**Hair Color:** Black
**Clothing:** Jean shorts and a blue tank top over a pink T-shirt with a star
**Gem Location:** Belly
**Fun Fact:** Stevonnie is the first human-Gem Fusion.
**Favorite Quote:** "Pretty cool, right?"